TELL THEM A STORY

*Using the Best Lessons
from Narrative Nonfiction
in Your Everyday Writing*

BEN RIGGS

THE-EFA.ORG

Copyright © 2020 by Ben Riggs
Cover and design © 2020 Editorial Freelancers Association
New York, NY

All rights reserved.
No part of this publication may be reproduced, distributed, or transmitted in any form or by any means, including, but not limited to, photocopying, recording, or other electronic or mechanical methods, without the prior written permission of the publisher, except in the case of brief quotations embodied in critical reviews and certain other noncommercial uses permitted by copyright law. For permission requests, write to the publisher at "Attention: Publications Chairperson," at the address below.

266 West 37th St. 20th Floor
New York, NY 10018
office@the-efa.org

ISBN paperback   978-1-880407-39-4
ISBN ebook   978-1-880407-40-0

Tell Them a Story: Using the Best Lessons from Narrative Nonfiction in Your Everyday Writing, by Ben Riggs

Published in the United States of America by the Editorial Freelancers Association.
Subject Categories: **LANGUAGE ARTS & DISCIPLINES** | Writing | Authorship | Nonfiction | Communication Studies

Legal Disclaimer
While the publisher and author have made every attempt to verify that the information provided in this book is correct and up to date, the publisher and author assume no responsibility for any error, inaccuracy, or omission.

The advice, examples, and strategies contained herein are not suitable for every situation. Neither the publisher nor author shall be liable for damages arising therefrom. This book is not intended for use as a source of legal or financial advice. Running a business involves complex legal and financial issues. You should always retain competent legal and financial professionals to provide guidance.

EFA Publications Director: Robin Martin
Copyeditor: Ruth E. Thaler-Carter
Proofreader: Heather E. Saunders
Book Designer: Kevin Callahan | BNGO Books
Cover Designer: Ann Marie Manca

*To my grandfathers, the patriarchs
of my storytelling genes—
To my team, the purveyors of storytelling—
To my Advanced Writer Workshop crews,
the future of storytelling—
To my wife, Emily, my favorite storyteller—*

I'm a better storyteller because of you.

Contents

What Hath Storytelling to Do with Nonfiction Writing?	1
Getting Started: Understanding Reports and Stories— and When to Use Them	5
Know Thy Theme: Connect to Readers and Stay on Target	11
Lead Well: Introducing Your Theme and Involving the Reader	15
Profluence: Keep Your Readers Moving	21
Don't Stop; End: How to Finish on Purpose and with Purpose	25
Bibliography	29
About the Author	31
About the Editorial Freelancers Association (EFA)	32

What Hath Storytelling to Do with Nonfiction Writing?

"Good writing transports us," writes Francis Flaherty, an editor at the *New York Times*. Hardly a writer or reader would disagree with him.

What hath story and storytelling to do with nonfiction? No matter what you're writing, the world of storytelling offers you a number of tools.

Let's begin with why story matters to any writer of any kind.

Flaherty belongs to a tradition of writers and editors from the school of writing referred to today as "narrative nonfiction." Some colleges offer it as "creative nonfiction." In the 1960s, before Flaherty covered his desk at the *Times* as the "Story Doctor," narrative nonfiction's first designation was "New Journalism."

What could have been new about journalism, which had its big break in the 1600s after the invention of the printing press? Enter Truman Capote. That's right: the author of *Breakfast at Tiffany's*.

In 1965, Capote published *In Cold Blood*, an account of a series of ghastly murders in the late '50s. His book became a bestseller, marked by factual accuracy shared through the transporting power of fictional prose. He called it a "nonfiction novel," and some have called it a literary experiment that "opened the way for a new kind of literature."[1] See

---

1 John Franklin. *Writing for Story*. Plume Books. New York. 23.

it as a writer's version of cross-pollination, maybe even a certain literary alchemy.

Before *In Cold Blood*, America's interest in nonfiction and journalism had already begun to grow. The breakneck speed of reporting captured readers' attention. With it came a writing technique that treated the reader more like a receptacle for information and headlines than someone to compel and entice with words and sentences from the first word to the final period. The inverted pyramid, the journalist's map for writing, ensured that a report's first paragraphs contained all the information readers would need, like a shirt in an overstuffed suitcase. This guaranteed readers' access to anything useful if the bottom paragraph had to be cut.

If readers did find the end of a story, it was often a carefully preserved replica of the first paragraph, just in case they forgot everything they read a moment earlier. This form of writing, along with the reading habits it required, made its way into magazines, advertising, and elsewhere. Reading styles changed, and most readers were seen as busy Monday-through-Friday go-getters who wanted the truth up front. Style and syntax were for weekend getaways in a novel.

Capote wrote for this growing audience of readers who desired factual writing, but he wanted to avoid succumbing to the facts-before-form, truth-trumps-technique writing characteristic of most reporting and nonfiction writing. He, and an emerging cohort of writers (Gay Talese, Tom Wolfe, Joan Didion, Norman Mailer), believed it was possible, if not necessary, to give audiences the truths of everyday life's blessed, boring, or brutal happenings *and* entertain them with the dynamism and qualities of good storytelling: character, theme, plot, action, scenes, concrete language, narrative distance, momentum, etc.

The techniques for compelling, literary writing now also belonged to the sports journalist, the political analyst, the magazine writer, the gardening columnist.

Capote and others saw that truth and technique could come together for the sake of the reader, and the result of that literary alchemy has been an explosion of Pulitzer Prize–winning storytellers, new genres like the personal essay, revitalized existing genres like the memoir and biography, and generations of new writers confident they can both inform readers with factual accuracy and captivate with literary strategy. What resulted wasn't just a "New Journalism"—what Talese coined "Literature of Reality"—but also an all-encompassing view of "story." Stories, and the tools and techniques to tell them, were now seen as part and parcel of everyday life.

As journalist and editor Jacqui Banaszynski writes, quoting a friend, Katherine Lanpher:

> Stories are the connective tissue of the human race, whether you are dissecting a school levy or South Korean politics. At the heart of every issue is a human element that leads to the three most beautiful words in the English language: *What happened next?* If you answer that question, you are a storyteller.

This perspective helps us step into our contemporary world and see that the tradition of "narrative nonfiction" isn't a hand-me-down from the '60s. It's a way to distill real life.

And we do this distillation now in a million places.

Our internet-infused existence has created countless new forms of and venues for writing—website copy, LinkedIn online posts and articles, travel blogs, food blogs, parenting blogs, product white papers, ebooks (like this one), not to mention thousands of emails—and the strategies attached to them are just as numerous: thought leadership, product clarity, value differentiation, content marketing, lead generation, brand awareness and credibility, customer upselling, customer loyalty, etc. In nearly all these cases, though, writers are *still* needing to know how to accurately distill real life accurately into words. Nonfiction. To accomplish all of these strategies, writers are *still* needing to write in order to entice, entertain, and compel readers. Narrative.

Even for genres that don't seem inherently "story-friendly," you can make many writing decisions that bring any reader to think, "What happens next?" Ideally, writing this way doesn't occur at the expense of the clarity and factual nature of nonfiction writing and its many forms.

You need tools and strategies to help you write nonfiction in a way that helps your readers—whoever they are—ask those three words, even if they don't know they're asking them. If you make certain writing decisions, they will find themselves traveling from sentence to sentence, paragraph to paragraph, having forgotten where they were before they started reading because they've been transported elsewhere.

As Flaherty wrote:

> Good writing transports us. We can glide down the Danube, peer into the Grand Canyon, feast at a roadside restaurant in Provence. Readers are greedy for life; their own is not enough. But they don't just hanker to see what others see; they want to feel what others feel. That journey is internal and invisible, but to readers it may be the most transporting trip of all.[2]

What does storytelling (narrative) have to do with reporting (nonfiction)? Everything.

---

2 Francis Flaherty. 2010. *The Elements of Story.* New York. HarperCollins. 15.

Getting Started: Understanding Reports and Stories— and When to Use Them

Narrative nonfiction is "the province of *factual prose* that is also *literary*— infused with the stylistic devises, tropes, and rhetorical flourishes of the best fiction . . ."[3]

Some writers hear the word "story" and imagine piles of anecdotes and long descriptions that keep readers from what matters: the truth. Perhaps a writer is writing a warning label that includes instructions for what to do if your child drinks bleach. How could a story be useful? If you find Johnny or Julie with the bleach-bottle cap, you need to act and read quickly, so a story isn't useful.

We need the brevity and immediacy of reports—beat journalism, breaking news—and their cousins—academic articles, instruction manuals, press releases, warning labels, and the like. But for most types of nonfiction writing that writers are writing, storytelling offers great resources for accomplishing most of the goals of nonfiction writing. In fact, most of the marketing, selling, persuading, and entertaining goals attached to today's writing finds its lineage in the bloodline of storytelling;

---

[3] Carolyn Forché and Philip Gerard. 2001. *Writing Creative Nonfiction*. Cincinnati. Story Press, 1.

namely, what prompts readers' curiosity, compels them to continue reading, and satisfies their needs as readers.

If you're writing leadership articles or recipe blogs or online-marketing copy, how can you use storytelling to your advantage? The best starting place is understanding the difference between reports and stories, and when to offer your reader either.

These two groups of sentences might be part of a marketing campaign for a "Train-Them-First" visiting first-aid training. The writer interviewed a family who benefited from the training and drafted these two paragraphs to highlight the value of the training.

1. Sally is a single mom of two teenage boys. She had an accident on Christmas Eve when she fell down her stairs carrying Christmas presents. Her wrist and neck were hurt by the fall. Her neck was stabilized by one of her sons while an ice pack was applied to her wrist by the other son. They knew what to do because they had been to a first-aid training that visited their local high school. Because their high school hosted a "Train-Them-First" first-aid training, they were able to spend Christmas together.

2. Watching her two boys open Christmas presents, Sally knew things could have been different today. The night before, Sally found herself lying at the bottom of her stairs. Carrying presents, she took a step and pitched downward. Acting quickly, one son held her head to prevent further neck injury. The other applied the comforting chill of ice to her wrist to keep swelling down. She knows the real gift this holiday is the "Train-Them-First" first-aid training hosted at her boys' high school. Without that, it would have been a different morning.

Both versions offer the same pieces of information, in about the same number of sentences and words. If we gave the first group of sentences to one reader in one room and the second group to another reader in a different room, they'd have the same information, right? But each reader would have a different experience. Why?

The first reader read a report and the second reader read a story. This reveals many of the differences between reports and stories.

Tell Them a Story

In his book *Murder Your Darlings*, Roy Peter Clark references the work of Louise Rosenblatt, an American professor and language researcher, who wrote about how the needs of readers changed the type of writing required to meet those needs. She identified one type of reader as looking for "efferent" writing and another looking for "aesthetic" writing. "Efferent" writing is no-frills writing, a one-stop shop for information, without a simile in sight. Efferent writing is the stop sign, the warning label, the school-closure announcement at the bottom of the TV screen. Aesthetic writing dwells on the other side of a spectrum from efferent. Aesthetic writing is metaphor-laden poetry and descriptive-heavy prose. They both serve readers well, as long as the writer has considered the reader's needs.

A parent with a child holding a bleach-bottle cap isn't going to run to read Shakespeare. Nor does a parent want to read the bottle and find the following:

> If your young one has found the elixir of stain-removal
> But the bottle's opening happened without your approval
> Don't descend into panic
> Avoid becoming frantic
> Your next task is rather quite simple
> And don't you worry, it's not a riddle
> Cast aside your current wants and plans for fun
> Grab a phone and dial 911.

What the reader needs in that moment should be fast, clear, quick, and directive: the purest form of efferent writing. That attempt at poetry is an example of aesthetic writing.

Let's return to the fake first-aid marketing copy. This intended reader is probably a school administrator, school-board member, or PTA parent. What do they need?

They have to *see* the need, *feel* the need, for this training. Which group of sentences created the experience of "seeing"? The second one.

That's the main difference between reports and stories: Reports tell us; stories show us. Or, as Roy Peter Clark writes, "The report points us there. The story puts us there."

If you want a school official to spend taxpayer money on first-aid training for students, that reader has to see Sally at the bottom of the stairs, see the two students jump to action, and see the family unwrap presents together the next morning.

One of the writer's first tasks is to discern what their reader needs—to be told information, or to be shown information? A writer must also discern their goals for the reader. Is any response or reaction desired? Discerning what the reader needs and your goals for a reader will change the writing decisions you make.

How do you know when you've written a report or a story? Let's return one more time to our two examples. What are notable differences, from a word-by-word and sentence-by-sentence perspective?

The first example—the report—offers static facts about Sally, her teenage sons, what happened, when it happened, and why it happened. As readers, we hover over the whole thing from 5,000 ft., rarely dropping down to come closer to the events. What keeps us as a distance is a series of static, fact-filled sentences.

What's notable about these fact-filled, static sentences and how they're organized? They have:

- a lot of linking verbs (is, were, been)
- three passive-voice constructions (were hurt by; was held by; was applied by)
- two occurrences of "because"
- one "were able to"
- repetitive sentence structure and similar sentence length
- disappearance of the writer

There is also no sensation of time or chronology—because we're being told information, it all seems to come to us in the same moment. We don't have much in the way of a "theme," and we wouldn't say we have any characters. That's OK, as long as that's what the reader needs, *and* the writer isn't anticipating much reaction or response from the reader.

These are the sentence and structure patterns that typically constitute a report.

The second example, the story, transports readers to a holiday morning, where we find Sally—who's become a character—watching her sons and reflecting; our "distance" from Sally isn't far. We're then taken to the night before, where we join Sally at the bottom of her stairs, and we're likely to feel the same loss of control: what it's like to miss a step. From her point of view, we see one son holding her head, we feel the ice pack's comfort, and we learn the boys' motives: to avoid further injury and keep swelling down. Where would two teenage boys learn that? First-aid training, of course. How does Sally, our main character, feel about it? It's this year's holiday gift.

What's notable about the sentences that make up this story? They have:

- numerous action verbs
- meaningful adjectives and adverbs (the comforting ice, the sons acting quickly)
- varying sentence structure and rhythm
- symmetry between beginning and end (Sally's reflecting)
- time as chronology
- writer as more of a narrator

These sentences and writing decisions give the reader access to a few key things to help them see:

- characters: Sally, the boys
- scenes: Christmas morning, bottom of the stairs
- theme: togetherness or family
- action: Sally watching and thinking, Sally falling, the boys acting
- motive: the boys' first-aid prowess

Whether the writer wants to "point" the reader to the information or "put" the reader in the story, to use Clark's words, will coincide with what the reader needs and their goals for the piece.

Let's imagine the "Train-Them-First" marketing materials continue, and the reader has finished the story draft. The reader has seen the value of the training. Now they need specifics about the training:

price, scheduling, contact information, etc. Should this take the form of a report or story? A report. This wouldn't be the time for a story.

By combining report and story writing, whether it's paragraph by paragraph or sentence by sentence, the writer of this marketing material would offer sentences that appeal to the reader as a whole person.

This is true for most writers: They can go back and forth between report and story, based on a reader's needs.

While certain genres and pieces of writing may need to trend closer to a report, like a warning label, writers can still ask themselves what paragraphs and sentences borrow from the realm of story and make a reader wonder, however subtly, *What happens next?*

Know Thy Theme: Connect to Readers and Stay on Target

It may seem ironic, but narrative nonfiction—and storytelling in general—could be boiled down to a simple equation:

Meaning + Emotion + Ongoing Action = Story

Before a story is about characters and scenes and descriptions and problems and resolutions, it must have these three things.

These three dynamics, or variables, can end up in nearly any piece of writing, but you need them to tell a story. And when it comes to meaning and emotion, what you need first is a theme.

A theme is a piece of writing's "big idea." It's the guiding principle that answers the question, "What is this piece really about?" Your theme allows you to instill meaning into your words and it helps readers connect to those words.

The concept of "theme" carries a lot of writing weight. It's a valuable tool from the world of storytelling, and it's a workhorse: It helps you connect to readers, discern what to keep in and remove from a piece, and shape how you begin and end a piece.

But it can be unruly, especially if you try to corral too many themes in one piece.

Connect to Readers

Deeper than the "big idea" is that the theme instills meaning into a story by addressing a **core or universal human experience**—something nearly every person can relate to. You may be writing or editing a blog or article about being a first-year teacher, but your theme may be fear of the unknown or finding your calling.

Your theme will create meaning for the reader *and* connect to a reader's emotions.

You haven't told a story if you haven't thought about a reader's emotions. Without engaging a reader's emotions, you won't connect with them.

Nearly all other goals we attach to our writing are preceded by connection—that moment a reader reads the first word and commits to continuing because they want to. Readers will exert their own energy to move from sentence to sentence, but only for so long. After a while, a reader who hasn't connected will move on elsewhere.

Equally important, if your theme is nonexistent or overrun by other themes, a reader will struggle to connect.

Most nonfiction writing has been written for specific audiences, and rightfully so, but even the most precise and specific audiences, even the most cerebral, need to connect to something deeper than what a piece is about at first glance: Everyone involves their emotions when they process information.

To make that connection, you have to identify your theme. To keep it from growing too complicated, find a one-word version: love, hate, fear, anxiety, loss, loneliness, community, betrayal, family, success, loss, etc. If you can't identify a one-word theme, ask yourself, "What is this *really* about?" This doesn't mean your writing has to mimic the emotive levels of a Pixar or Disney movie (unless warranted). An article on structural engineering likely won't bring readers to tears, and shouldn't. By situating your piece of writing on the back of a theme, however subtle the theme is, you can inject deeper meaning into even the most prosaic and pragmatic of nonfiction pieces.

By situating your piece of writing on the back of your theme, you can inject meaning into even the most pragmatic of nonfiction pieces, and connect to a wide range of readers by involving their emotions, however subtly.

But tread carefully: Many writers have succumbed to the temptation to highlight more than one "big idea," which leads to cluttered and overcrowded writing.

Stay on Target: Keep Your Main Theme the Main Theme

An effective theme is noncompetitive. You want to do your best to stick to one theme and keep it from competing with others.

In this sense, your theme helps you decide what to keep and what to remove; if something doesn't help advance, or clarify, or point back to your theme, it's liable to distract the reader and clutter your writing. Omit it.

Think of your theme as your story's bouncer. It stands at the doorway of your writing, letting in those words, phrases, and sentences that you need. A nicely dressed aside paragraph or profound metaphor doesn't belong simply because it's impressive. Having a theme helps writers do the difficult work of "murdering your darlings" or as Strunk and White advise, "omitting needless words."

"But what about my voice?" some writers ask. "If my theme brings me to cut everything not relevant to it, will anything be left that makes me, me?" Knowing your theme doesn't sanitize your writing. It keeps it from floods of needless modifiers, parades of endless dialogue, out-of-place details, and self-indulgent sentences.

Your theme helps you make writing decisions that enhance your writing by sticking close to it, particularly with how you begin your piece (the lead), maintain momentum (profluence), and finish (your ending).

Here are a few key strategies to stay on target.

1. Use descriptive writing when it's most relevant. This is valuable for addressing something useful, and dangerous as an exhibition to show readers your powers of description. If you're writing

about burnout, use your word count to describe the frazzled mental state of someone working eighty hours a week, or panicking about inevitable daunting piles of work.
2. Choose metaphors and similes (comparative language) that reveal your theme. If you're writing about burnout, consider writing about a father's volcanic anger or a friend's snuffed-out energy level.
3. Use action verbs that point to your theme. This will keep the readers moving, it will help you use language that "shows," rather than "tells," and it will keep readers connected. If you're writing about burnout, consider the host of verbs at your disposal: flicker, burn, smoke, smolder, fume, extinguish, etc.

Thinking about theme is an indisputable way to unlock your writing so you can offer great storytelling. Themes offer writers great opportunities to fill in the first two variables for a story: meaning and emotion. They also provide a great writing tool to help readers ask, "What happens next?"

Lead Well: Introducing Your Theme and Involving the Reader

Few tasks are as frustrating for writers as crafting the first words—or lead—of a piece of writing.

Jack Cappon referred to the lead as "the agony of square one." For many, leads are the Medusa of writing, turning countless writers to stone who gaze at that blank screen or page for too long.

Leads: More than an Introduction

Leads, it's often said, introduce the reader to the theme. We learn this in our composition and writing classrooms. It's good advice, but it often reduces a lead's job to introducing a piece and hoping that readers carry on purely out of self-interest: "Reader, meet theme. Theme, reader." The lead's role is more dynamic. A well-written lead, in its many forms, *involves* the reader.

The sentences in a lead have a task different from every other sentence afterward. While every sentence after the lead keeps readers involved, the lead sentences first *entice* them. They exist to heighten intrigue and invite readers to invest time. This is less of a dilemma for book writers, but for pieces between 600 and 7,000 words, writers should consider the lead as "the doorway into every text. Its job, *never a minor one*, is to draw the reader over the threshold" (emphasis mine).[4]

What's in a [Great] Lead?

The best leads provoke curiosity and questions that the following sentences begin to answer. Great leads are written with the understanding that readers themselves contribute to their own reading experiences.

There is one question, though, that writers and editors must help readers avoid asking: "Where's this going?" If a reader asks this before they reach the second paragraph, it's over.

As William Zinsser wrote in *On Writing Well*, "The most important sentence in any article is the first one. If it doesn't induce the reader to proceed to the second sentence, your article is dead."

That said, the best leads have a static task—introduce—and a dynamic task—involve the reader.

Types of Leads

There are many types of leads that get the job done, and a master has wielded each type with precision. Four effective types to learn and cycle through are the "I need more," "set the scene," "double-take," and "fact" leads.

I Need More: These leads are engaging, but tricky to execute. When done well, readers think, "I'm going to need to know more about *this*." These feel explosive, and they're engineered to carry the energy of intrigue in a precise direction. They come with a flashing "warning" sign, though: Be wary of thinking you've dropped a humdinger in a reader's lap when it's a dramatic dud.

---

4 Francis Flaherty, 201.

"Several years ago, a fifteen-year-old boy answered the side door of a house where I once lived, and was murdered, shot twice by one of five people—two women and three men—who had gone there to steal a pound of cocaine."[5]

This is from Ted Kooser's essay *Smalls Rooms in Time*. He writes about his former home, but his theme is about the effects of time's brutality on nostalgia. It's subtle: Wrapped in alarming news, his former home steps onto the stage, and we're curious and buy in.

Set the Scene: Scene leads supply a sturdy setting and guide the reader's gaze toward a specific focus. These appeal to readers' senses by establishing where they are while showing why they're there in the first place.

"On the second floor of an old Bavarian palace in Munich, Germany, there's a library with high ceilings, a distinctly bookish smell and one of the world's most extensive collections of Latin texts. About 20 researchers from all over the world work in small offices around the room. They're laboring on a comprehensive Latin dictionary that's been in progress since 1894. The most recently published volume contained all the words beginning with the letter P. That was back in 2010."[6]

Written by Byrd Pinkerton of NPR, there's a lot of potential for a report to meet us here. Instead, we can almost smell the books in this otherwise-obscure library—and now we're interested.

Double-Take: Double-take leads, as Flaherty calls them, emerge at the intersection of two unlikely things—an Amish man selling refurbished Apple products, for instance—and inspire the same questions that probably made it worth writing about in the first place. These almost

---

5   Ted Kooser, "Small Rooms in Time," in *The Best American Essays*, 2005. Susan Orlean, ed. New York: Houghton Mifflin, 2005, 100.
6   Byrd Pinkerton, "The Ultimate Latin Dictionary: After 122 Years, Still At Work On the Letter 'N,'" NPR.org, National Public Radio, May 14, 2016.

guarantee questions that require further reading. Just make sure you deliver on your promises.

> "It took 60 years before they found each other and amassed enough proof to overcome skeptics. But a handful of families who survived the Holocaust are responsible for having a German army officer recognized for saving hundreds of Jews from extermination during World War II."[7]

Alison Leigh Cowan of the *New York Times* used that double-take lead for a story that deserves it. Wouldn't you keep reading to find out more?

Fact: Fact leads are the most docile, but pack plenty of power to provoke by using the fact that the world is big and mysterious. Fact leads deliver the world's oddity, and occasional charm, to a reader's doorstep. These leads typically offer some mind-blowing fact or figure. This doesn't imply, though, that every big number is worth the real estate of first sentences. Suffice it to say, when you find it, you'll know.

> "The dead will eventually outnumber the living on Facebook, according to a new study whose authors want us to think more about the importance of preserving our collective digital histories."[8]

Rachel E. Greenspan of *TIME* leveraged this fact lead well. How do we know? You're still thinking about how staggering that news is.

Make Your First Words Count

What's the best lead for your piece? Unless you're under the gun for time, try two or three leads and consider which one foots the bill the best. In

---

7 Alison Leigh Cowan, "60 Year Later, Honoring an Unlikely Hero of the Holocaust," nytimes.com, *The New York Times*, March 28, 2005.
8 Rachel Greenspan, "On Facebook, the Dead Will Eventually Outnumber the Living. What Does That Mean for Our Histories?" time.com, *TIME*, April 30, 2019.

most cases, you'll find one that doesn't feel forced. If you feel that way about them all, set them aside to polish later.

If you feel particularly flummoxed, write a bland lead, draft your body and conclusion, then return to your lead. Nothing says you *must* craft the lead before everything else. Many leads stutter and stammer because a writer hasn't narrowed their gaze to a single theme. If you still feel out of sorts, you may need to do further reporting or research.

How long should it be? Leads can grow with the piece's overall word count, but there's no need to keep anyone waiting for long. Readers want to know why they're there and should continue reading. Herein lies the glory of the well-written lead: Writers can find a compelling harmony between pointing readers in the direction they'll be reading and coaxing them to be inquisitive. Great leads almost leave readers believing it was their idea to keep reading. But you know better: You prompted the questions *and* you spread out your answers.

Before you walk away from your draft thinking it's ready for publishing, check that you haven't spent a paragraph or more clearing your throat. Writers often find their targets after they've warmed up their confidence and fingers by writing several sentences. Read the first paragraph, then the second or third. If the second or third paragraph say the same thing as the first but better, cut the first paragraph. Your readers will thank you for making those first words count by asking, "What happens next?"

Profluence: Keep Your Readers Moving

Coined by novelist John Gardner, "profluence" is the momentum that carries a reader along to the end of a piece.

Among the tactics and habits a writer ought to develop, knowing how to move readers along at a smooth pace while keeping them engaged with careful descriptions is the secret sauce to any written piece.

Why Profluence?

Think about the last thing you enjoyed reading. What possessed you to continue to give your time to reading its words and linking its ideas together until that final period?

Perhaps you felt it was well-written or it continued to satisfy your curiosity. I'm willing to bet the real reason you felt it was well-written and you thought it satisfying is because the writing never slowed down or stalled anywhere.

Of the two dominant jobs of the writer (movement and description), movement is crucial. Without movement, the reader grows tired and underwhelmed, and is willing to put your writing down at any moment.

The Temptation

We've all been arrested when an author's precise, alarmingly detailed descriptions put us in the midst of the action or setting. Read a page from Annie Dillard's *Pilgrim at Tinker Creek* or C.S. Lewis's *The Chronicles of Narnia*, and share that experience. As the reader, we love these moments. Being transported from your current station to another country, world, or existence is what makes superb storytelling.

Like all good stories we read, we want to write them ourselves, so we take to our paper and our keyboards, and we hammer away at a piece laced with precise, fine-tuned descriptions of this thing or that place. But what starts out as an exercise to ignite a reader's imagination often turns into a moment similar to someone grabbing you and jerking your head toward a window, demanding "Look!"—only for you to be disappointed not to see what all the hubbub was about, while having the discomfort of someone forcing your gaze.

Strike the Balance

Great writing maintains a healthy balance of both momentum and description.

A piece that's only momentum—with no additional commentary, explanations, vivid scenery, etc.—moves at breakneck speed, allowing the reader to ingest only what's on the surface. As Francis Flaherty says about writing that moves too fast, "The story will be spare and colorless, just like an old-time telegram." It's like being on a tour bus that never stops, only increasing its speed, with the tour guide providing all the information in one breathless trip.

A piece that's only description is a tour bus that's parked at Starbucks between sites while the guide explains every detail and nuance of the Starbucks logo. Soon enough, someone is going to be tempted to forcibly remove the driver and slam on the gas pedal.

Effective writing is neither a speeding nor a parked tour bus; rather, it moves along the streets of sentences, slowing down only when helpful and useful to visitors.

Tell Them a Story

Ways to Establish Profluence

1. **Use Right-branching, Cumulative Sentences:** Begin most of your sentences with the energy of "who and what"—right-branching—instead of backing into the action with long, clunky strings of introductory prepositional or adverbial phrases. Add modifying phrases and clauses to the sentence after the subject and verb—cumulative. This allows the writer to say something definitive first, then provide descriptions.

2. **Use Punctuation to Modify the Reader's Pace:** Roy Peter Clark offers great advice about this—"Let punctuation dictate the pace and space of the sentence." Get to know what punctuation does not just grammatically, but stylistically. Become familiar with the ways you can use various pieces of punctuation to introduce pauses and breaths for the reader. Remember: The reader begins with the capital letter and gathers momentum until crashing headlong into a period. Punctuation not only provides a means of attaching or setting off information, it also allows you to pause and pivot the reader when you want them to encounter that information.

3. **"Sweat Over Your [Relevant] Descriptions":** Drawing from the advice in the chapter about theme, "sweat over your descriptions" is more insight from Flaherty. It doesn't mean "Sweat over (every one of) your descriptions." Descriptive writing slows down your reader, so you want to make that slowing down count. If you're writing about a car accident you were in with your significant other, best not to spend sentences describing the steak you had during the date before the accident.

4. **Find and Focus on the Action:** Action verbs explode with imagery and vividness; they're the dynamite of the sentence. Everything else in your sentences controls the blast. Find the action inherent in what you're writing about, even if it doesn't appear lively at first. Even a stopped car has a world of engineering and chemistry occurring underneath the hood. A well-placed action verb can quicken a reader's pace through sentences of dense, layered descriptions. If many of your sentences sound like a report, a good action verb won't let you or your reader down.

Finally, be wary of the idea that everything you've written matters to the reader. This is, perhaps, the toughest lesson for a writer, but it's necessary. You're going to write beautiful, dynamic descriptions you're proud of, but don't let that fool you into thinking that everyone wants to read them. As Stephen King wrote:

> In many cases when a reader puts a story aside because it got boring, the boredom arose because the writer grew enchanted with his powers of description and lost sight of his priority, which is to keep the ball rolling.[9]

Creating profluence in a piece of writing is every writer's duty. No reader wants to sit there, stalled out in a writer's ego trip or uncertainty. Your theme helps provide the variables of meaning and emotion; profluence provides the variable of ongoing action.

As your readers move through your sentences and encounter that delicate balance of description and movement, they'll encounter answers to their question of "What happens next?"

---

9 Stephen King, *On Writing*, New York, Pocket Books, 2000, 178.

Don't Stop; End:
How to Finish on Purpose
and with Purpose

We all know the sensation of slamming into the final period of a piece like a car into a brick wall. We've also read endings that make us feel like passengers being promised a landing as the plane continues to circle. Neither is pleasant. The first fails to signal that the ending is approaching, and the other fails to arrive; two jobs of a quality ending. Every writer must learn to end well. If the lead provides a first impression, the ending provides a lasting one.

Flipping the "Inverted Pyramid"

The inverted pyramid trained journalists to arrange information from the most important at the top to the least important at the bottom. Why? The telegraph. Journalists sent stories in bursts, with the most-important piece of information first, in case the line failed. Later, the same technique proved useful to ensure stories would fit when space was at a premium. Stories were written and edited on paper, and a typographer then set them in type. A story's type had to fit a designated amount of space on the page. If it took up too much room, the best way to cut the excess was to trim from the bottom.

Today, we don't use the telegraph, we don't use lead type, and space can be almost infinite. We have a delete button, and proportional type or spacing, and writing online means we're not confined to a certain amount of space. The ending is no longer on the chopping block, at least when writing in environments other than print. Even with telegraphs and type tucked away, though, the skittish shadow of the inverted pyramid still darkens many pieces of writing.

More Than Déja Vu

A quick quiz about the role of the ending, or kicker, might reveal that a good portion of us believe the ending is where we "recap" or "summarize" what we've written about.

Using the ending to merely "summarize" amounts to nothing more than forcing a moment of déja vu upon the reader.

Zinsser in *On Writing Well* said that the weakness of using the ending to summarize what's been written is that it "signals to the reader that you are about to repeat in compressed form what you have already said in detail." In other words, most endings tend to say, "Dear Reader, I don't trust you to remember what you've read, so here's a recap in condensed form."

If the ending isn't intended to summarize, then what is it for?

What Makes for a Good Ending?

Good endings supply a practical and a poetic service to the reader. A good writer will conclude a piece *on purpose* and *with purpose*.

Ending on Purpose

1. **Signal the End:** A good ending will signal that the end is near. You may be thinking, "But wait, don't they *see* that it's the final paragraph?" Yes—but don't rely on that white space to do the heavy lifting expected of your writing. It might help to imagine there's no white space below the final paragraph to tell the reader things are ending. Now, how will your writing do that for the reader? For

most nonfiction pieces, you can't always rely on having a resolution, but you can still create a sense of finality through a personal reflection, a character's epiphany or revelation, or even looking to what "might be" in the future. A great, satisfying way to signal the end to your reader is to offer an echo from the lead. Circling back to something in the beginning provides the reader with the satisfaction of symmetry.

2. **Arrive on Time:** Like a movie that could have ended an hour earlier, some writing can outlast its audience. This problem arises when writers don't ask themselves, "What do I want to say?" *and* "Have I said it?" There's no magic number of sentences or paragraphs to indicate when the reader has had too much; the ending should be intuitive as you move through the writing process. The best way to avoid overshooting your reader's bandwidth is not to skimp on the editing, rewriting, and—most assuredly—cutting. Do the hard work of divorcing your ego from your words and step away for a little while. Come back fresh and reread your piece, looking for words that keep the reader from the ending. Ask others to read it. When no one asks, "When is this going to end?" you've hit your mark.

Ending with Purpose

1. **Reinforce the Theme:** Although we're not looking to "summarize," we do want to point readers back to why they were reading in the first place—but this doesn't have to be a literal restating of the theme. If you've written something using numerous themes, you'll find yourself at an impasse when you reach the moment to craft your ending. Anyone who's tried to emphasize more than one theme in their endings knows how muddy things can get. To avoid this, draft your ending first. Discern your destination and reverse-engineer everything else to meet there. This will not only ensure your piece will reach its desired end, it will also help you get a leg up on how to craft your lead.

2. **Make It Ring:** The best endings echo in readers' ears and minds long after they have finished. Strunk advised us to "Place emphatic words at the end." This is true for entire pieces of writing as well. The ending used to be treated like lowly swampland, but the

ending is prime real estate to entertain and inspire the reader. The bottom of your piece should offer some of your best writing. Don't front-load all of your creativity into the first sentences. Surprise the reader with some of your best work at the end.

Think of endings as the "grab bag" a host gives to guests—something that says to the recipient, "Thanks for sticking around." Of course, the more spectacular the grab bag, the more likely they are to remember you and your party.

Great endings matter because readers matter. They deserve our best from the first word to the final period. Having provided that, writers can wrap up any piece of nonfiction writing confident that they will have a reader who won't regret asking, "What happens next?"

Bibliography

Banaszynski, Jacqui. "Stories Matter" in *Telling True Stories: A Nonfiction Writers' Guide from the Nieman Foundation at Harvard University*. eds. Mark Kramer and Wendy Call. New York: Plume, a division of Penguin Books. 2007.

Clark, Roy Peter. *Murder Your Darlings: And Other Gentle Writing Advice from Aristotle to Zinsser*. New York: Little, Brown Spark. 2020.

_____. *Writing Tools: 50 Essential Strategies for Every Writing*. New York: Little Brown and Company. 2010.

Cowan, Alison Leigh. "60 Years Later, Honoring an Unlikely Hero of the Holocaust." nytimes.com. https://www.nytimes.com/2005/03/28/nyregion/60-years-later-honoring-an-unlikely-hero-of-the-holocaust.html (accessed April 6, 2020).

DeSilva, Bruce. "Endings" in *Telling True Stories: A Nonfiction Writer's Guide from the Nieman Foundation at Harvard University*. eds. Mark Kramer and Wendy Call. New York: Plume, a division of Penguin Books. 2007.

Flaherty, Francis. *The Elements of Story: Field Notes on Nonfiction Writing*. New York: HarperCollins. 2009.

Franklin, John. *Writing for Story: Craft Secrets of Dramatic Nonfiction by a Two-Time Pulitzer Prize Winner*. New York: Plume, a division of Penguin Books. 1994.

Forché, Carolyn, Philip Gerard, eds., *Writing Creative Nonfiction: Instruction and Insights from Teachers of the Associated Writing Programs*. Cincinnati, Ohio: Story Press. 2001.

Greenspan, Rachel. "On Facebook, the Dead Will Eventually Outnumber the Living. What Does That Mean for Our Histories?" time.com. https://time.com/5579737/facebook-dead-living/ (accessed April 6, 2020).

King, Stephen. *On Writing: A Memoir of the Craft*. New York: Pocket Books. 2000.

Kooser, Ted. "Small Rooms in Time," in *The Best American Essays*, 2005. Susan Orlean, ed. New York: Houghton Mifflin. 2005.

Pinkerton, Byrd. "The Ultimate Latin Dictionary: After 122 Years, Still At Work On the Letter 'N,'" NPR.org. https://www.npr.org/sections/parallels/2016/05/14/476873307/the-ultimate-latin-dictionary-after-122-years-still-at-work-on-the-letter-n (accessed April 6, 2020).

Strunk, William, Jr. *The Elements of Style: The Original Edition*. Mineola, New York: Dover Publications, Inc. 2006.

_____ and E.B. White. *The Elements of Style with Revisions, an Introduction, and a Chapter on Writing*. New York: The Macmillan Company. 1959 (with several subsequent editions).

Zinsser, William. *On Writing Well: The Classic Guide to Writing Nonfiction*, 30th-anniversary edition. New York: HarperCollins. 1976, 2006.

About the Author

Ben Riggs is founder of RiggsWriting LLC; associate editor with Good Comma Editing; and lead instructor with Good Comma Classroom LLC.

A graduate of the Ohio State University (2006) and a former expat resident in Cancun, Mexico, Riggs has been a member of the Editorial Freelancers Association since 2017. He enjoys writing, and loves writing about writing.

(Editor's note: Versions of some chapters have been published in the EFA's *Freelancer* newsletter.)

About the Editorial Freelancers Association (EFA)

Celebrating 50 Years!
Dedicated to the Education and Growth
of Editorial Freelancers

The EFA is a national not-for-profit — 501(c)6 — organization, headquartered in New York City, run by member volunteers, all of whom are also freelancers. The EFA's members, experienced in a wide range of professional skills, live and work all across the United States and in other countries.

A pioneer in organizing freelancers into a network for mutual support and advancement, the EFA is now recognized throughout the publishing industry as the source for professional editorial assistance.

We welcome people of every race, color, culture, religion or no religion, gender identity, gender expression, age, national or ethnic origin, ancestry, citizenship, education, ability, health, neurotype, marital/parental status, socio-economic background, sexual orientation, and/or military status. We are nothing without our members, and encourage everyone to volunteer and to participate in our community.

The EFA sells a variety of specialized booklets, not unlike this one, on topics of interest to editorial freelancers at the-efa.org.

The EFA hosts online, asynchronous courses, real-time webinars, and on-demand recorded webinars designed especially for freelance editors, writers, and other editorial specialists around the world. You can learn more about our Education Program at the-efa.org.

To learn about these and other EFA offerings, visit the-efa.org and join us on social media:

Twitter: @EFAFreelancers
Instagram: @efa_editors
Facebook: editorialfreelancersassociation
LinkedIn: editorial-freelancers

www.ingramcontent.com/pod-product-compliance
Lightning Source LLC
Chambersburg PA
CBHW071549080526
44588CB00011B/1849